Author:
Fiona Macdonald studied history at
Cambridge University and at the University of East
Anglia. She has taught in schools, adult education
and universities and is the author of numerous
books for children on historical topics.

Artist:
David Antram was born in Brighton, England,
in 1958. He studied at Eastbourne College of Art
and then worked in advertising for fifteen years
before becoming a full-time artist. He has
illustrated many children's non-fiction books.

Series creator:
David Salariya was born in Dundee, Scotland.
He has illustrated a wide range of books and has
created and designed many new series for
publishers both in the UK and overseas. In 1989,
he established The Salariya Book Company. He
lives in Brighton with his wife, illustrator Shirley
Willis, and their son Jonathan.

Editor:
Michael Ford

Published in Great Britain in 2004 by
Book House, an imprint of
The Salariya Book Company Ltd
25 Marlborough Place, Brighton BN1 1UB

Please visit the Salariya Book Company at:
www.salariya.com
www.book-house.co.uk

ISBN 1 904642 11 X

A catalogue record for this book is available
from the British Library.

Printed and bound in Belgium.

Printed on paper from sustainable forests.

Avoid sailing with Christopher Columbus!

...and this is all the thanks I get!

The Danger Zone

Written by
Fiona Macdonald

Illustrated by
David Antram

Created and designed by
David Salariya

BOOK HOUSE

Contents

MA	MB	MC
MD	ME	MF
MG	MH	MM
MN	MO	MR
AB	MT	MW

Introduction

The year is AD 1492. The place is Palos, a harbour town in south-west Spain. You are a bright young lad, but your parents are poor – your father repairs boats and your mother sells shrimps in the market place.

Now you're ten years old, it's time you found a job, to help support your family. Some boys in your street are already working, running errands and washing pots and pans at the inn. Others are training for skilled jobs as blacksmiths or carpenters. A few have joined the crews of fishing boats.

But you don't want to do work like this! Secretly, you have another ambition. You dream of being an explorer and having amazing adventures in faraway lands. Who knows? One day, you might have the chance to sail on a long ocean voyage. But before you go on board ship, think carefully. Are you ready to leave your family, suffer months of hardship and danger – and possibly lose your life?

So you want to go to sea

Spain borders the Mediterranean Sea and the wide Atlantic Ocean. It has busy harbours all around its coast. For centuries, Spanish people have relied on the sea to make a living. Many have become sailors and fishermen, but others have not left dry land. They've built ships, sewn cloth to make sails, hammered iron into anchors, twisted ropes, knotted nets and crafted wooden chests and barrels. They've laboured to unload ships' cargoes and built huge warehouses to store them. With all these different jobs on shore to choose from, are you sure that you still want to go to sea?

Why travelling by sea is best:

TRAVELLING BY SEA has many advantages, especially over long distances or when carrying bulky cargoes. Journeys by land (below) can be difficult and dangerous.

CROSSING RIVERS can be difficult. You'll find broken bridges and slippery stones.

IN SUMMER, you'll suffer from thirst, heatstroke and exhaustion.

YOU'LL HAVE TO FIGHT off fierce bandits that lay in wait to rob travellers.

IN WINTER, you'll face frostbite and sink up to your neck in snow.

TAKE CARE not to fall off your horse, or into a pothole.

Why do you want to explore?

You know that exploration is the latest craze among clever people – and merchants seeking their fortunes. Ships from nearby Portugal have made voyages along the coast of Africa, searching for a sea-route to India. You've seen rich people wearing precious silks and jewels brought back from Far Eastern lands and you've smelled the rich Arabian perfumes they wear! Now there's a rumour in town. A stranger has arrived at the monastery, to talk to monks and scholars there. His name is Columbus and he's planning a voyage.

Eastern treasures:

CUSTOMERS all over Europe will pay high prices for goods brought from Asia and the Middle East.

PEPPER

SILK

MEDICINES

SCENT

GOLD AND PRECIOUS STONES

RIVALS! The kings of Spain and Portugal (above) both want to conquer lands in Asia and control the profitable trade in silks, jewels and spices.

IMAGO MUNDI. Columbus used a book called *Imago Mundi* (meaning 'Picture of the World') to support his ideas that the Atlantic could not be a wide ocean.

All explorers are fools! They'll fall off the edge of the world!

Iceland

ATLANTIC OCEAN

Europe

Africa

Columbus so far:
1451 Born Genoa, Italy.
1465 Sails merchant ships in Mediterranean.
1476 Moves to Portugal and makes plans for voyage to the East.
1484 Asks King John of Portugal for money. King John refuses.
1485 Moves to Spain.

Handy hint

Remember, for centuries scholars have argued that the world is round, even though it looks flat!

RECENT EXPLORATION.
In the past few years (above), explorers have already sailed north-west, beyond Iceland, and south-west, to remote islands in the Atlantic Ocean.

It says in *Imago Mundi* that the Earth is round.

Yes...and between the end of Spain and the beginning of India lies a narrow sea that can be sailed in just a few days.

How would you pay for the voyage?

Approaching the rich:

MOST EXPLORERS need money to go on their expensive voyages. There are a few tricks you should know.

FLATTERY (above). Praise the Queen's noble birth, generous nature, and pious reputation.

NATIONAL PRIDE (right). Tell the King that he'll win lasting fame for backing your voyage.

olumbus is making plans for an extraordinary adventure.

He believes that he can reach Japan – the easternmost country known to Europeans – by sailing west across the Atlantic Ocean. But Columbus has no money to pay for his voyage. Buying just one ship is extremely expensive and, for safety, he really needs two or three. Columbus must persuade rich people to help him. Over five years ago, in 1486, he asked the king and queen of Spain for money. They turned him down. But Columbus never gave up hope and earlier this year (1492) he asked again. This time, he's been lucky! Queen Isabella has said she'll pay for his voyage!

Turned down? You could:

INHERIT. If you're lucky, an elderly relative will leave you a fortune when they die.

BE ENTERPRISING. Sell shares or persuade businessmen to invest in your voyage.

BE WARLIKE. Spend a year as a soldier and take prisoners. They'll pay vast sums to be set free.

10

11

How would you prepare your fleet?

Food for the voyage:

SHIP'S BISCUITS are hard, tasteless and full of weevils!

SALT OR PICKLED MEAT. Scrape the mould off before you eat.

DRIED PEAS are either too hard or too mushy.

CHEESE is very smelly and full of worms.

OCEAN FISH is fresh-caught, but it looks very strange and may not be edible!

WINE AND WATER. At sea, wine easily turns to vinegar and stored water becomes very salty.

Ship mates:

ABOUT 90 SAILORS have agreed to serve as crew. There are also 2 captains, 3 masters, 3 pilots, 3 boatswains, 3 stewards, 3 caulkers (to mend leaks) and a doctor – plus some government officials, who may be spies.

ow exciting! Columbus has chosen your town as the home base for his fleet. He arrived last night, carrying orders from the king and queen. These say that the people of Palos must find ships for Columbus, equip them with crewmen, food and drink, and have them ready to sail – all within 10 weeks! The townsfolk are not very happy about this. And they believe that Columbus's voyage will end in disaster.

Sea air

Fortune

Riches

Money

Gold

The language barrier

MAKE SURE your interpreter speaks the right language. Columbus is taking an Arabic-speaker with him to the Caribbean!

Handy hint

Thud!

Don't let any women on board – they're meant to be unlucky!

So the townsfolk do not co-operate. But one sea-captain, Martin Alonso Pinzon, realises that this voyage is his great opportunity to win fame and fortune. He takes charge, stocks the ships and recruits a rough and ready crew – including you!

Spices
Fame
Fortune
Treasure
Adventure
Silver
Sandy beaches

13

Could you handle a sailing ship?

Columbus's three ships:

SANTA MARIA.
Designed to carry cargo,
she's strong but slow,
and hard to control when
out on the open sea.

Santa Maria

olumbus is taking three ships on
this voyage – the *Pinta*, the *Nina*,
and the *Santa Maria*. Like all
other vessels, they are made of
wood and are powered by the
wind trapped in their sails.

Handling a sailing vessel is not an easy task.
It takes strength and experience to raise and
lower the heavy sails and real courage
to climb the tall rigging. If too
many sails are hoisted, the
masts might crack, or the
whole ship might capsize.
But if there are too few
sails, the ship cannot steer
a safe course and will
drift dangerously at
the mercy of the sea.

Whoosh!

Pinta

PINTA. A caravel (ship
with a sleek, narrow hull)
fitted with big square
sails. She's the fastest of
Columbus's three ships.

Nina

NINA. A small, light
caravel, fitted with triangular
sails. She rides the waves
and should be easy to
handle, even in storms.

14

Handy hint

Learn to sew! One day, your life may depend on being able to mend a sail.

LOOK OUT. Don't get caught out by calms, or your ship will drift aimlessly.

Be a safe sailor!

DON'T GET CAUGHT up in the ropes used to raise and lower the sails.

FIRM GRIP. Don't fall from the rigging that holds the masts in place.

TIE the sails down firmly or they'll flap in the wind and might rip and blow away.

HOLD ON TIGHT when you climb the mast to reef (shorten) the sails in a gale.

15

Which way would you steer?

You head west, across the Atlantic Ocean. Columbus thinks there's land in that direction – and not without reason. Plants, unknown in Europe, have been washed up on west-facing shores. Columbus has read books which make him think that Japan is only about 4,400 km away (it's 15,000 km further!). He calculates that he should reach it quickly. But just in case he doesn't, he's decided to keep two logbooks. One, for himself, records the true course he's steering. The other shows a safer route, closer to land, to calm the fears of crew members like you.

To help you navigate:

AN HOURGLASS measures time and calculates how far you've travelled westwards every day.

Hourglass

AN ASTROLABE is used to work out your latitude (distance north or south of the equator).

Astrolabe

LOGBOOK. Make a note of your ship's journey in a logbook at the end of each watch.

Logbook

LOOKOUT. Send someone up to the crow's nest to spot hazards.

A COMPASS is used to check the ship's course.

DIVIDERS (metal pincers) measure precise distances on charts and maps.

Dividers

THROW a line and weight to check the depth of the water.

Compass

Traverse board

TRAVERSE BOARD. The helmsman marks each change of course by sticking a peg into a board.

Put your back into it! The ship's flooding!

I can't stand pumping the bilges!

Handy hint

Keep a diary of your voyage. If you get home safely, you can publish it and make your fortune!

Columbus's world

Spain

Where Columbus thinks Japan is

ATLANTIC OCEAN

...and the real world

Where Japan actually is

Spain

PACIFIC OCEAN

PACIFIC OCEAN

Columbus does not know that the continent of North and South America and the vast Pacific Ocean lie between him and Japan.

Could you cope on board?

The crew's duties:

Pumping bilge-water

Cleaning the deck

Mending sails

Checking ropes

Inspecting cargo

Mending leaks

Life at sea is tough. You have to keep the boat 'shipshape' (neat and safe), but it is crowded, cold, damp, smelly and infested with fleas. It leaks and has to be pumped out every day. There are no beds or chairs, except in Columbus's private cabin, so you have to sleep anywhere you find space. You can't get used to the system of watches – four hours on duty, then four hours rest – so you feel tired all the time. Some older sailors amuse themselves by gambling and quarrelling – and criticising Columbus.

EATING. Forget table manners. The cook spreads food out on deck and sailors help themselves.

WASHING. When it's fine, you can wash in sea water. But there's no soap and sailors do not shave.

THE TOILET is just a wooden seat fixed over the side of the ship. But when the weather's bad, find a dark place in the hold.

ITCHY? Ask other sailors to help comb the lice from your hair.

UGH! The bilges are usually full of slimy, smelly water.

RATS. Most ships are infested with these vermin.

OBEY ORDERS, or you'll feel this whip on your back.

18

Handy hint

Sqwark!

Sleep up on deck. It's cleaner and healthier than down below.

Where's my private cabin?

PRAISE THE LORD! On board ship, each day begins and ends with a religious service. The first is at 3 am, when a cabin boy sings a hymn.

Would you lose hope?

t's over two months since you sailed away from Spain and there's still no sight of Japan. The crew start to grumble that Columbus has made a mistake in his calculations. You wonder whether you are all doomed to die? Everyone on board has done his best to keep a lookout for land, but with no success. On 10th October, the crew of your ship, *Santa Maria*, organise a protest to confront Columbus. They say that the voyage west has gone on long enough and demand that he turn the ships round to go home. He refuses, but the men are still unhappy. Will there be a mutiny soon?

Hopeful signs of land:

MIST AND CLOUD. This sometimes gathers above islands.

BIRDS flying overhead. Most don't go far out to sea.

SEAWEED. It often grows in shallow waters close to land.

SHELLFISH and other creatures that like to live on beaches.

BRANCHES that have fallen off seaside trees.

SMELLS of sweat and sewage mean that people are nearby.

A GLOW on the horizon might mean houses, lights and fires.

Could you survive on shore?

Land at last! It's Friday, 12th October. For the first time in months, you are standing on solid ground. You've just scrambled ashore, along with Columbus and his bodyguard. He's already claimed these islands for Spain! Now he's marching towards some local men. They seem friendly, but very surprised. In the distance, you can see their village. It has tall, round houses, thatched with grass.

But if this is Japan, why aren't people wearing silk robes. Where are the jewels you hoped to find and the palaces roofed in gold? You can see that Columbus is puzzled too. He's captured seven local men to guide his ships in search of treasure and spices. They call these islands 'Bahama' – not Japan!

This isn't what I had in mind.

What you'll find as you explore:

HAMMOCKS. Slung between trees, they make comfortable beds – if you keep still!

TOBACCO. Taino people on the nearby island of Cuba breathe its smoke. Ugh!

YAMS. These huge roots are very nourishing. But how do you cook them?

IGUANA. These green, meaty lizards are best roasted. Are you hungry enough to eat one?

PEPPERS AND CHILLIES. Test your tastebuds with these favourite fiery flavourings.

MAIZE. You need good strong teeth to enjoy a meal of these golden-yellow corn cobs.

Would you get home safely?

You've spent two months exploring. Columbus has landed on two big islands, which he's named Cuba and Espanola. He's very excited, because he has seen people wearing gold necklaces on Espanola. This convinces him that Japan can't be far. But, like many of his tired crew, you're feeling homesick – and you've caught a nasty tropical disease. Captain Pinzon sails away in the *Pinta*, saying that he's going back to Spain. But the next day is Christmas Day and you are looking forward to a special meal. Then disaster strikes! The *Santa Maria* runs aground and water pours in. You have to abandon ship!

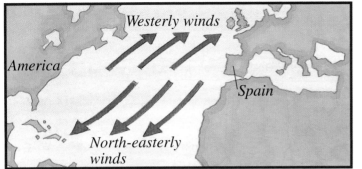

North-easterly winds blew Columbus's ships from Spain towards America. But he won't be able to sail back unless he heads north, where westerly winds blow.

Handy hint

Make your voyage at the right time of year! Avoid the hurricanes that blow in spring and autumn.

What next?

LOAD as much as you can from the wreck of the *Santa Maria* onto the little ship *Nina* (left).

YOU DON'T have room for all the crew, so leave some men behind to build a settlement (right).

USE WOOD from the wreck to build a fort (left), to protect the men left behind from attack.

TAKE SOME TAINO people (right) back to Europe with you, to show the king and queen.

SAY FAREWELL to the men left behind and set sail in the *Nina* (left).

SAIL as fast as you can! You don't want the *Pinta* to reach Spain before you, and win all the glory!

Would you make more voyages?

THE SECOND VOYAGE. Columbus finds his first settlement destroyed by Tainos. He also hears that the local Carib people (below) are cannibals!

The ship *Nina* finally reached Palos harbour on 15th March, 1493. Soon after, Columbus received a hero's welcome from the king and queen, who eagerly agreed to pay for another voyage. They hoped he'd conquer more land, find more gold and convert local peoples to Christianity. You sailed with Columbus on that second voyage, and on

THE THIRD VOYAGE. Columbus makes slaves of the Tainos. The Spanish in the new settlement on Espanola rebel against him. Columbus gets very ill and is accused of fraud. He is sent home to Spain as a prisoner, in disgrace.

THE FOURTH VOYAGE. Columbus's ships are worm-eaten and his men are very weak. They are stranded on a sandbank in Panama, then marooned on Jamaica for a year.

Columbus's later voyages:

→ Second voyage (1493-1496)
→ Third voyage (1498-1500)
→ Fourth voyage (1502-1504)

Cuba

Espanola

Jamaica

Central America

South America

two more since then. But was this really a good idea? You've visited beautiful countries, but you've also seen much death and disaster. Columbus quarrels with the local people and treats them like slaves.

Handy hint

Pity the Carib and Taino people. Thousands die from diseases brought by Spanish settlers, such as the common cold.

I wonder if I should have been a carpenter.

Would it all be worthwhile?

It's now 1504 and Columbus has made his last voyage. He's back home in Spain, tired, ill, bitter, angry – and deeply disappointed. His expeditions have exhausted him, but he's still as determined as ever. He spends his days trying to win back power and glory and still thinks that he reached the continent of Asia and the islands of Japan. He's sad – and mistaken – but don't forget: his voyages changed our view of the world forever.

So, looking back at the time you spent with him and all the adventures you shared, do you think it was all worthwhile? If you were given the chance again, would you really want to sail with Christopher Columbus?

Columbus's final years:

1) ARCH ENEMY. The King of Spain appoints Columbus's rival, Nicolas Ovando, as governor of Espanola.

2) AMERICA is named after rival explorer, Italian Amerigo Vespucci, who sailed in 1499 and 1501.

3) RICH REWARDS? Columbus receives just one-fiftieth of the gold found on Espanola, not one-tenth as he hoped for.

4) COLUMBUS'S LETTERS to the Spanish king, begging forgiveness and favour, are thrown away.

5) DEATH. After Columbus dies in 1506, later explorers prove that many of his ideas were wrong.

6) COLUMBUS'S SON is made Admiral of the Ocean Sea and Governor of the Indies in his place.

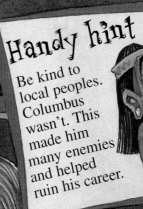

Handy hint

Be kind to local peoples. Columbus wasn't. This made him many enemies and helped ruin his career.

Why do they doubt me? One day they'll call me a great explorer!

Glossary

Astrolabe Metal disc with a pointer that helps sailors work out their latitude.

Bilges The lowest part of a ship's hold.

Boatswain The ship-board manager.

Calms Dangerous weather at sea when the wind drops and ships drift with the tides.

Capsize Overturn.

Caravel A sailing ship with a sleek, narrow hull.

Carpenter Someone who makes things out of wood.

Caulkers Workers who mend leaks by filling gaps in ships' wooden hulls with old rope and tar.

Crow's nest The lookout post at the top of a ship's mast.

Dividers Metal pincers used for measuring distance on a map.

Enterprising Daring, energetic and keen to make money.

Flattery Extravagant praise.

Frostbite Damage to the skin because of extreme cold.

Helmsman The man who steers a ship.

Hourglass A glass jar filled with sand that trickles slowly from top to bottom. Used to measure time.

Hurricanes Violent storms.

Iguana A large animal, rather like a lizard.

Inherit Gain something from an older relative when they die.

Latitude Distance north or south of the equator.

Lead A heavy weight tied to a rope.

Marooned Left alone to starve on an island.

Master An expert sailor.

Monastery A place where monks live and work.

Mutiny A rebellion by soldiers or sailors.

Pious Loyal to one's religion.

Pothole A hole in a road.

Reef To shorten sails.

Rigging Ropes that hold a ship's masts in place.

Sea-legs Experience of going to sea.

Ship's biscuit A hard, dry mixture of flour baked with water.

Shipshape Neat and safe.

Watch A period of duty on board ship.

Yams Tropical plants with swollen, fleshy roots.

Index